Rudy the Red Pig

With love from Rudy!

*Catherine Ritch Guess
September 17, 2011.*

Written by
Catherine Ritch Guess

Drawings by
Jason Haynes

Painting by
Rachel Oke

CRM BOOKS
Publishing Hope for Today's Society

Inspirational Books • CDs • Children's Books

CRM BOOKS, P.O. Box 2124, Hendersonville, NC 28793

Visit our Web site at www.ciridmus.com

Rudy the Red Pig, "Rootin' for Reading" and "Racing for Reading" are trademarks of
    Rudy & Friends Reading Pen, Inc.

The Rudy the Red Pig Series books and toys are used by special licensing arrangement through
    Rudy & Friends Reading Pen, Inc., PO Box 68, Indian Trail, NC 28079

Visit Rudy's website at rudytheredpig.com

Printed in the United States of America
First CRM BOOKS Edition: September 2006
10 9 8 7 6 5 4 3 2 1

10 digit ISBN: 1-933341-13-0
13 digit ISBN: 978-1-933341-13-2
LCCN: 2006907400

Early every morning, Randy, Cory and Jean arrive at the
Red Pig Café to cook for all the customers
who love to come there and eat. One morning,
they saw something very strange beside the dumpster
at the back of the parking lot. It was a pink baby pig,
so puny that no one wanted it.

"You poor little thing," said Jean, stooping beside the pig. "You look hungry. I need to fatten you up." She picked up the baby pig, carried him inside the restaurant and sat him on a stool.

"Here's a nice Cherry Lemon Sun-Drop for you to drink. I'll be right back with some food." The baby pig imagined a slop bucket filled with cherries and lemons, and longed for some corn.

He watched Jean in her bakery, where she was famous
for her delicious desserts, as she began to stir something in a bowl.

"Look! A bowl of scrumptious corn nuggets just for you. My grandsons love these," said Jean as she sat the bowl on the counter. The little pig's face lit up with delight.

After several weeks of corn nuggets, the pig grew much bigger. He also grew much pinker. Every morning he buried his face in his bowl, slopping up the food as pigs do. Then one morning, he saw Randy in the kitchen cooking bacon and sausage links.

The little pig
became so
frightened that
he closed his eyes
and began
to shake.
The stool began
to wobble from
side to side.

Then it began
to spin,

slowly at first,

with the pig's
color getting darker
and darker with each spin.

It went faster
and faster
until it flung
the little pig
up into the air.

The little pig
opened his eyes
and began to
squeal with all
his might.

"Squee,
Squee,
Squeee!"

His tail
began to propel,
causing
him to hover
above the
stool and the
countertop.

Randy and Cory looked out the
kitchen window in shock.

Jean came running from the kitchen to see what was causing all the commotion. "Awwww!" she exclaimed as she threw her hands to her face.

She finally decided to try to catch the pig. When she moved her hands, her face was covered in floured handprints.

"Ha, ha, ha!" laughed the pig as he pointed at Jean's face.

PLOP! When he laughed, he fell straight to the floor.

Cory picked up the pig and placed him back on the stool,
noticing that his color had grown from a bright
pink to a deep red.

Randy handed the pig the Cherry Lemon Sun-Drop.
"Here, take a sip of this. That was quite a fall."

"I've never seen a pig that could fly before," said Jean.

"Or laugh," added Randy.

"You must be a very special pig. Even your color is different from other little pigs. Why don't you stay here and we'll take good care of you?" Cory asked.

"Yes," agreed Jean. "You can be our new mascot. Rudy. Rudy the Red Pig."

"How do you like that, Rudy?" asked Cory.

Rudy closed his eyes, thinking how wonderful it was to be special and wanted, and to have his very own family.

Suddenly,
the stool began
to wobble and spin again.

Soon Rudy was back
in the air, propelling his tail
and hovering over
the countertop.
"Whee!" he squealed.

All of the customers began to clap and cheer. "Yeah, Rudy!"

"You're Number One!"
They were all very glad to see
the little red pig have a new home.

That evening before Randy and Cory left the Red Pig Café, they made Rudy his very own pigpen beside the dumpster.

He lay down, wallowing out a spot for himself in the mud,
and went to sleep. Rudy was sure he would have pleasant dreams
about his family, and corn nuggets and Cherry Lemon Sun-Drop.

Randy, Cory and Jean went home for their own restful night's sleep
so they could come back and feed Rudy
and all the Red Pig Café customers the next day.

Coming
November 2006

Rudy and the
Magic Sleigh

To Kevin Stradley,
Caleb Lyle,
Carson Lyle
and Jacob Thorn

The Red Pig Cafe "Grands"

Catherine Ritch Guess is the creator of Rudy the Red Pig and author of the Rudy the Red Pig Series. She is also a composer, with 3 CDs of original compositions and arrangements, and the author of 14 fiction and non-fiction titles, as well as the White Squirrel Parables, another children's series. Catherine spends her time between North Carolina's Blue Ridge Mountains and her native home of Union County, NC.

Jason Haynes was born in Charlotte, North Carolina where he has lived his entire life. Jason graduated from David W. Butler High School and went on to graduate from UNC Charlotte. He grew attached to sketching when he was 12 and has been drawing ever since. Jason hopes to continue following his interest in art for years to come.

Rachel Oke graduated from David W. Butler High School in Charlotte, North Carolina in 2004. She currently attends the University of North Carolina at Pembroke, and is pursuing a degree in Art with a concentration in ceramics. She hopes to open her own pottery studio, and continue painting and illustrating.

Rudy the Red Pig lives at the Red Pig Café in the Carolina Mall of Concord, NC where Jean, Randy and Cory Lyle feed him regularly. He is the mascot of "Rootin' for Reading" – a non-profit campaign to promote reading and writing throughout America, and to replenish the shelves of the school libraries of the Gulf that were destroyed during Hurricane Katrina.

Rudy is "officially" licensed through Rudy & Friends Reading Pen, Inc., PO Box 68, Indian Trail, NC 28079.

Visit Rudy at rudytheredpig.com to become a member of the Li'l Rooters and/or the Li'l Oinkers.

You may e-mail him at rudy@rudytheredpig.com